Farm to Table

Milk

ANN O. SQUIRE

Children's Press®
An Imprint of Scholastic Inc.

Library of Congress Cataloging-in-Publication Data
Names: Squire, Ann.
Title: Milk / by Ann O. Squire.
Description: New York, NY : Children's Press, 2017. | Series: A true book | Includes bibliographical
    references and index.
Identifiers: LCCN 2016030827| ISBN 9780531229330 (library binding) | ISBN 9780531235522 (pbk.)
Subjects: LCSH: Dairy products—Juvenile literature. | Dairy
    farming—Juvenile literature. | Milk—Juvenile literature.
Classification: LCC SF250.5 .S7727 2017 | DDC 636.2/142—dc23
LC record available at https://lccn.loc.gov/2016030827

Front cover: Holstein dairy cows
Back cover: A bottle and glass of milk

Find the Truth!

Everything you are about to read is true *except* for one of the sentences on this page.

Which one is **TRUE**?

T or F Dairy cows produce much more milk each day than is necessary to feed a calf.

T or F Most milk and dairy products are produced on small family farms.

Find the answers in this book.

3

Contents

THE **BIG** TRUTH!

Finding Nutrients

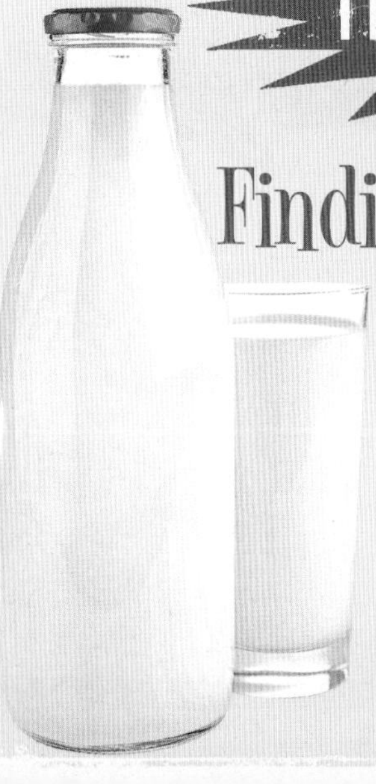

A bottle and
glass of milk

4

Holstein cow

Dairy farmer

From Farm

1 Dairy cows are led into a milking parlor where they are hooked up to milking machines. The milk flows through the machines to a collection jar. When the jar is full, the milk is transferred to a refrigerated storage tank.

3 Workers take the temperature of the milk and test for certain medications, bacteria, and other harmful substances. Milk with any issues is dumped.

2 An insulated tanker truck takes the milk to a factory.

to Table

4 The approved milk is heated to a certain temperature and then rapidly cooled in a process called pasteurization. This kills bacteria and helps the milk last longer.

6 The milk is bottled and sent to either grocery stores or factories, where it will be turned into dairy products such as yogurt, cheese, and butter.

5 The milk is put in a machine that separates the cream from the milk. The cream is mixed back into the milk in different amounts, depending on the desired fat content. Then the milk is homogenized, or mixed so the fat is well distributed.

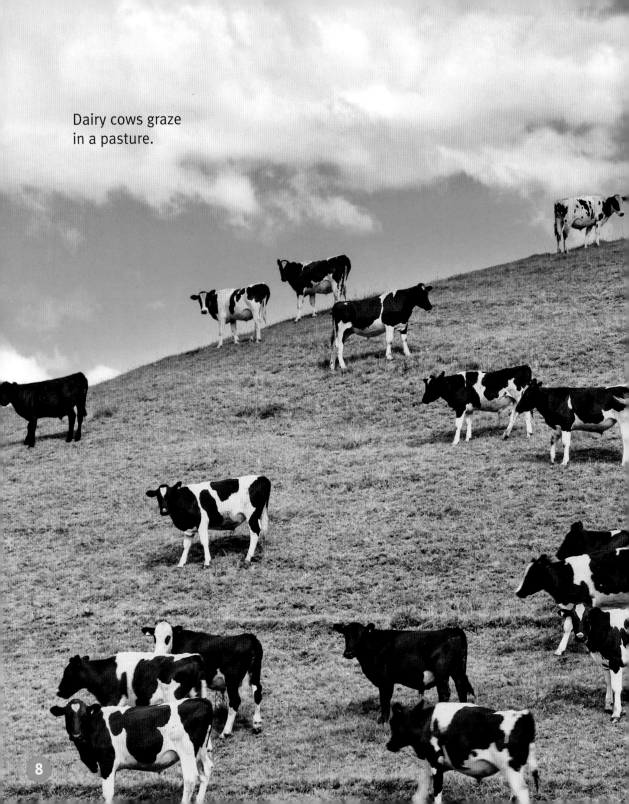

Dairy cows graze
in a pasture.

CHAPTER 1

Where Does Milk Come From?

When you pour a glass of milk, eat yogurt, or add a slice of cheese to your sandwich, where do you imagine those foods came from? Maybe you picture a herd of cows grazing on a hillside. As the sun sets, the cows head into a big red barn at the top of the hill. There, they are milked by the farmer and farmhands. However, many of today's dairy cows, goats, and other milk-producing **mammals** live different lives on much bigger farms.

The black-and-white Holstein cow is known for its ability to produce a lot of milk.

Dairy in History

Dairy cows are descended from wild oxen. These oxen were **domesticated** in southwestern Asia more than 10,000 years ago. Goats were domesticated at about the same time. It is likely that people domesticated these animals to have a ready source of meat. But they learned that cows and goats could give them milk, too.

A wall carving in Egypt from between the 24th and 22nd centuries BCE shows workers milking a cow.

How do we know that ancient people kept dairy cows and goats? In addition to paintings, archaeologists have studied pottery vessels unearthed in Europe, Africa, and Asia. The vessels are between 4,000 and 7,000 years old. In them, scientists have been able to detect traces of fat from the milk and milk products that had been stored inside. This tells them that the vessels were used to store diary products.

Preserving Milk

Raw milk spoils very quickly unless it is kept cold. Ancient people needed to find ways to make it last longer. This led them to create processed or changed forms of milk, such as yogurt, cheese, and butter. These products can be stored much longer without going bad. They also helped reduce the issue of **lactose intolerance**. For some people, the sugar in milk, called lactose, is difficult to digest. This was an issue in ancient times as well as today. Cheese and other dairy products are often easier to digest.

Processing milk can produce a wide variety of dairy products.

A young woman leads her cow home.

Cows in the Colonies

Europeans began settling in colonies in the Americas in the 1500s and 1600s. It didn't take long for them to decide they needed livestock, and the first cattle on the continents arrived in ships from Europe. For many years, most people kept one or two cows or goats of their own to produce milk for their families.

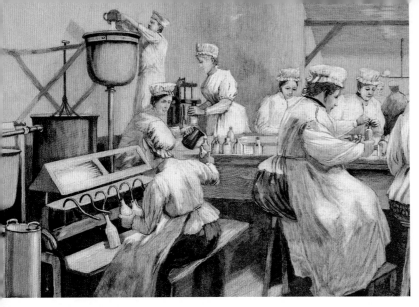

Workers filter cream and bottle milk at a factory in Denmark in about 1897.

As the population grew in the next centuries, more people moved into cities. Crowded urban communities did not have space for dairy cattle. As a result, rural farms had to produce more milk and ship it longer distances. By the 1800s, farmers were developing cattle breeds that produced large quantities of milk. Inventions such as milking machines, refrigerated tanks for transportation, and processing and bottling equipment changed the industry. Safer milk was produced and shipped faster than ever before.

Not Just Cows

All mammals produce milk. In the United States, people usually consume cow milk. But around the world people use milk produced by many other animals. Sheep, goats, buffalo, and camels are common milk producers. Yaks, horses, reindeer, and donkeys are less common examples. Why choose these animals over a cow? Goats can thrive in areas with poor soil. Camels can live in dry environments. Buffalo do well in wet, tropical regions. Yaks can live in high, mountainous areas. These are all places where cows might not survive.

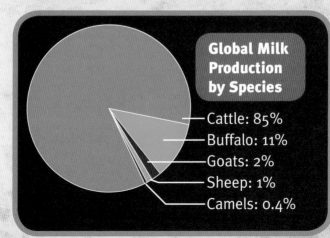

Global Milk Production by Species

- Cattle: 85%
- Buffalo: 11%
- Goats: 2%
- Sheep: 1%
- Camels: 0.4%

A camel

Dairy cows standing in stalls to eat

Modern Dairy Farming

Dairy farming is now a gigantic industry. Few American families today keep their own cow or other animal for milk. Instead, most people buy their milk at the grocery store. Only one-quarter of American farms have more than 100 cows, but these farms produce 86 percent of our milk. Some large dairy farms have hundreds or even thousands of cows.

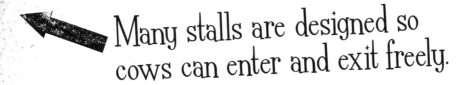

Many stalls are designed so cows can enter and exit freely.

A Dairy Cow's Day

On large farms, dairy cows typically spend their days in indoor stalls or on feedlots, munching corn and alfalfa. Two or three times a day, the cows are led into the milking parlor, where they are attached to milking machines. After each cow has been milked, the milking machine is taken off. Then the cow's **udder** is cleaned and swabbed with disinfectant to prevent disease. Most cows are milked a few times each day. On average, a cow produces about 70 pounds (32 kilograms) of milk a day. This is about 8 gallons.

Milking machines are hooked up directly to a cow's udder.

Milk tankers must be cleaned regularly. This makes sure any milk carried in the tank stays fresh and free of bacteria.

Collecting the Milk

As each cow is milked, its milk flows into a collection jar. When the jar is full, the milk is transferred into a large storage tank where it is cooled and kept refrigerated. Every day or every other day, a huge tanker truck arrives at the farm. It picks up the milk and takes it to a factory for processing. The tankers are insulated to keep the milk cold during transport.

A thermometer keeps track of milk's temperature during pasteurization at a small facility in Haiti.

Each shipment of milk is first tested. The tests check for temperature, **antibiotics** and other drugs, bacteria, and other things. If the tests reveal problems, the milk may be rejected. Next, the milk is spun in a machine called a centrifuge. This separates the milk and cream. Then vitamins A and D are added. After that comes **pasteurization**. The milk is heated to a specific temperature and then cooled. This kills bacteria and helps the milk stay fresh longer.

Whole or Fat-Free?

To produce different types of milk, the cream that was separated out in the centrifuge is mixed back in. The amount of cream added depends on the desired fat content, whether whole milk (about 3.5% fat), 2% fat, 1% fat, or fat-free. Next, the milk is **homogenized**. This distributes the milk fat evenly throughout the milk. If the milk is not homogenized, the fat separates and rises to the top.

Most grocery stores carry a range of milk options.

Final Steps

After processing, the milk may be bottled for sale. It may also be made into products such as yogurt, cheese, and butter. At the bottling plant, the milk travels through pipes to automated packaging machines. Milk is usually packaged in paper, plastic, or glass containers. These are stamped with a date to show how long the milk will stay fresh.

What Forms of Milk Are Sold?

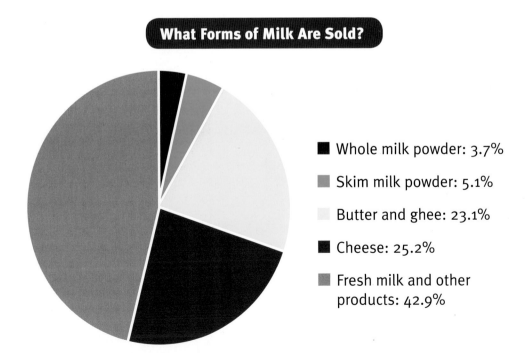

- Whole milk powder: 3.7%
- Skim milk powder: 5.1%
- Butter and ghee: 23.1%
- Cheese: 25.2%
- Fresh milk and other products: 42.9%

The Holstein: A Milk Machine

Most dairy cattle are a breed called Holsteins. They are easily recognizable by their black-and-white markings. Holsteins are known for their amazing milk production. The average Holstein cow can produce nearly 24,000 pounds (10,886 kg) of milk in a year. That's about 2,800 gallons of milk. Some cows produce even more. In 2015, a Wisconsin Holstein named Gigi (pictured below) set an astonishing record: 74,650 pounds (33,861 kg) of milk in one year. That's an average of more than 200 pounds (91 kg) per day.

Finding Nutrients

All mammals, including humans, start out on a diet of milk as they nurse from their mothers. But humans are the only animals that continue to drink milk after childhood. Drinking milk throughout life has a lot of benefits. But it can also cause problems for some people.

The Benefits of Milk
Milk is a good source of calcium, vitamin D, and protein. The United States Department of Agriculture (USDA) recommends 2 to 3 cups of milk or dairy products per day. This helps build strong bones and teeth.

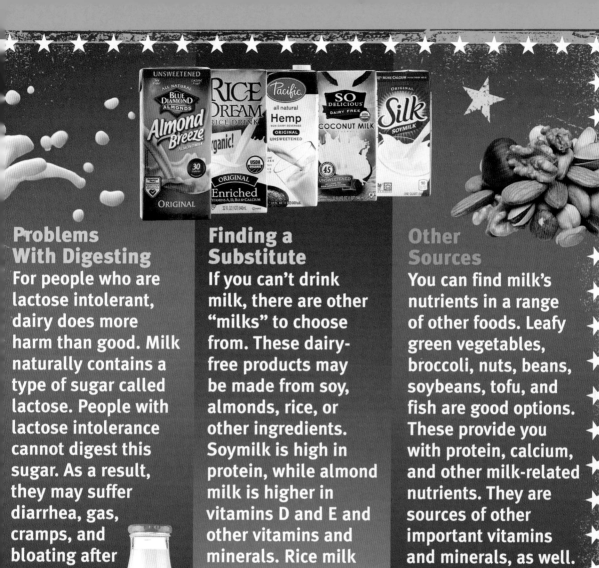

Problems With Digesting

For people who are lactose intolerant, dairy does more harm than good. Milk naturally contains a type of sugar called lactose. People with lactose intolerance cannot digest this sugar. As a result, they may suffer diarrhea, gas, cramps, and bloating after they eat dairy products.

Finding a Substitute

If you can't drink milk, there are other "milks" to choose from. These dairy-free products may be made from soy, almonds, rice, or other ingredients. Soymilk is high in protein, while almond milk is higher in vitamins D and E and other vitamins and minerals. Rice milk is the least likely to cause allergic reactions, but it's low in nutrients.

Other Sources

You can find milk's nutrients in a range of other foods. Leafy green vegetables, broccoli, nuts, beans, soybeans, tofu, and fish are good options. These provide you with protein, calcium, and other milk-related nutrients. They are sources of other important vitamins and minerals, as well.

CHAPTER 3

Problems in Dairyland

A dairy cow's life might not be exactly what you had imagined, but at first glance it doesn't seem too bad. The cows have ample food, shelter, and medical care. In return, they give us milk. As it turns out, however, intensive dairy farming can be harmful to the cows, to the people who drink their milk, and even to our planet.

Between 1983 and 2013, world milk production increased by more than 50 percent.

A cow lies with her recently born calf.

Cows and Calves

For a cow to produce milk, she must first have a calf. A cow's pregnancy lasts about nine months. On some small farms, calves remain with their mothers after birth. But on large dairy farms, calves are taken away within a few hours or days of being born. This can be very stressful to both mother and baby. The stress is reduced if the calf stays and nurses for a few months. Farmers lose profit, however, if much of their cows' milk goes to calves.

Another source of stress to dairy cows is being pregnant often. When a cow's milk begins to dry up, she is usually bred with a bull so she will become pregnant again. After a few years of many pregnancies, the cows become worn out. Their milk production begins to go down. At this point, they are often sold off for hamburger meat.

Many dairy cows have a calf about once each year.

Corn and soy feed comes in the form of pellets.

Making More Milk

Through much of history, dairy cattle were kept in pastures where they grazed on grass. A diet of grass is not high in nutrients. Grass-fed cows produce only enough milk to nourish a calf. Today, dairy cattle are often given a high-protein diet of corn and soy. The protein helps cows produce more milk, which increases a farmer's profit. The feed also removes any need for grazing outdoors. Some dairy cattle are confined to indoor stalls. Others are kept in open covered lots.

Some dairy farmers may also give their cows growth **hormones**. These hormones are copies of a hormone that naturally occurs in cows. Hormone treatments boost milk production even further. A cow that has taken hormones may produce an average of 11 pounds (5 kg) of milk per day. This is two times the amount an untreated, grass-fed cow produces. Most U.S. dairy farmers no longer use hormones, though it is not against the law to use them.

Hormones are given as injections.

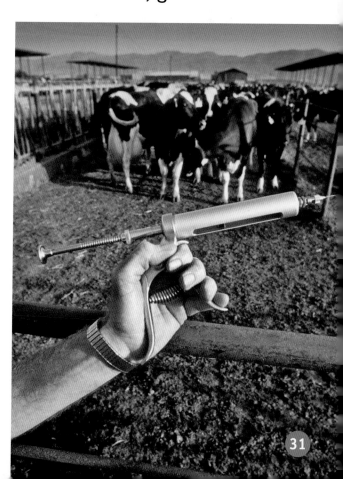

Because milk from cows treated with antibiotics cannot be sold, farmers use antibiotics only when necessary.

Producing a lot of milk is very hard on a cow's body. Many dairy cows, whether they are treated with hormones or not, suffer from a painful infection called mastitis. To treat this and other diseases, cows may be given antibiotics. Traces of the antibiotics can remain in the milk even after it is processed. This can cause health problems in people who drink the milk. For this reason, any milk that is found to have traces of antibiotics is disposed of before it is sold.

Passing Gas

Cows and other grazing animals have stomachs designed to break down grass and other plant fibers that are difficult to digest. As they digest their food, cows produce a gas called methane. This gas makes its way into the atmosphere when the animal passes gas or burps. Methane contributes to climate change and the warming of our planet. Experts estimate that the world's livestock release an astonishing 100 million tons of methane each year.

3 Some energy escapes back into space.

2 Methane and other gasses in the atmosphere trap the energy. This warms the planet.

1 Energy from the sun reaches Earth.

What's the Solution?

To make money, most dairy farmers must push their cows to produce large quantities of milk. They cannot reserve much milk for their cows' calves. And when a cow's milk production starts to go down, the farmer must remove her from the herd. Is there a way for farmers to treat cows more humanely and still make a profit? The answer is yes, but it requires many changes.

Few farmers today have time to milk their cows by hand.

Humane Dairy Farming

For a more humane way of life, dairy cows must be allowed to be outdoors, grazing on grass. They should not be given growth hormones. And they must be allowed time with their calves after birth. All these changes mean happier cows, but they also mean that each cow will produce less milk to sell. For farmers to make the same profit, they have to charge more for each gallon of milk they sell.

Timeline of the Life of a Dairy Cow

1 day
A calf is born and is usually taken from its mother in its first few hours.

6 to 8 weeks
The calf drinks milk or milk replacer, which is like baby formula. It gradually switches to solid food such as hay, feed, and grass.

Dan Gibson runs a special farm in New York State. His Jersey cows receive no growth hormones and graze on grass. Calves stay with their mothers for several months. Thirteen of Gibson's cows produce about as much milk as two Holsteins on a **conventional** dairy farm. Gibson's milk sells for roughly $7 per half gallon, compared to about $3 for conventional and $4 for **organic** milk. Unfortunately, this can make Gibson's milk unaffordable for many people.

2 years

The young cow has its first calf and begins producing milk for the farm.

4 years

The cow has reached full size. It has a calf about once a year.

5–15 years

The cow no longer produces much milk and is removed from the herd.

If more consumers demand milk and dairy products from humanely treated animals, more farmers will change their practices. As more farmers produce animal-friendly products, the supply will go up. Perhaps in time, prices may go down, making the products affordable to more people. Such changes will drive a real and positive impact on the lives of dairy cattle. ★

Dairy products from humane farms are not yet affordable to everyone. They are also not yet available in all stores.

What's In Milk?

When you drink a glass of milk, what exactly is going into your body? Here's the breakdown of 1 cup (245 grams) of whole milk:

Major Vitamins and Minerals

Nutrient	Percent of Daily Needs
Sodium	4
Potassium	9
Vitamin A	11
Vitamin B12	18
Vitamin D	31
Calcium	28
Magnesium	6
Phosphorus	21
Thiamin	7
Riboflavin	24

What's in Whole Milk?

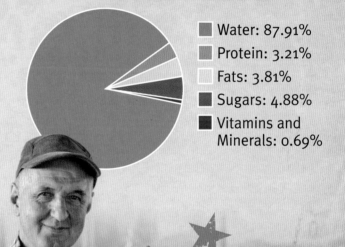

- Water: 87.91%
- Protein: 3.21%
- Fats: 3.81%
- Sugars: 4.88%
- Vitamins and Minerals: 0.69%

DAIRY AND YOU!

You can make milk and dairy products or dairy substitutes a healthy part of your daily diet. Here are some pointers on how!

DRINK (AND EAT) UP!

The USDA recommends having 2 to 3 cups of milk each day. But you don't have to stick to drinking milk. Yogurt and cheese also count toward your daily dairy. One cup of milk is equal to about one regular container of yogurt. For cheese, one serving is two cheese slices or 2 cups of cottage cheese.

FIND HEALTHY CHOICES

Some dairy products are healthier than others. Dairy desserts, flavored milk and yogurt, and similar products are often high in unhealthy ingredients such as sugar. If you drink milk substitutes, check the nutrition label for things like protein, calcium, and vitamin content. The higher these numbers are, the better. Look for the amount of sugar, too. The healthiest options are unsweetened.

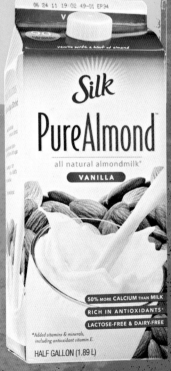

CHECK LABELS

Animal Welfare Approved (AWA) labels guarantee the dairy cows were treated humanely. Organic farms are held to higher standards, too. Check the ingredients list for information on whether particular ingredients come from organic sources.

Is High-Fat Dairy Better Than Low-Fat Dairy?

Milk and dairy products are an important part of our diet. But what kind of milk should we drink? For decades, the USDA has recommended we choose low-fat or fat-free options. Other experts have argued full-fat dairy might be the better choice. Both sides say their options are healthier.

Which side do you agree with? Why?

Yes We should choose high-fat dairy!

Obesity, or being very overweight, is a growing problem in the United States. So is diabetes. Diabetes is a disease in which a person's body cannot control blood sugar levels. Studies have shown that **people who consume whole milk and other high-fat dairy have a lower risk of obesity and diabetes**. In one 15-year study, participants who consumed high-fat dairy were 46 percent less likely to develop diabetes than those who had fat-free dairy. Scientists aren't sure why this is true. One reason may be that the fats and protein in whole milk make people feel fuller longer, so they eat less. The fats may also help cells function. Plus, reduced-fat foods often do not taste as good as full-fat foods. To make up for this, **companies often add sugar, salt, or other ingredients to reduced-fat dairy that are unhealthy**.

No We should choose lower fat options!

Saturated fat may be connected to increased risk of heart disease. **Whole milk and other high-fat dairy products are high in saturated fat**. To cut down on this kind of fat, people should choose low-fat or fat-free dairy options whenever possible. Also, low-fat and skim milk are full of nutrients, but they have fewer calories than whole milk. **Skim milk even has higher levels of calcium than whole milk**. This makes skim milk a useful tool for people who are trying to lose weight by cutting calories. People can avoid unhealthy additives such as salt and sugar by checking a product's label. That way, consumers can have the health benefits of low-fat dairy without the unhealthy added ingredients.

Percent of the world's milk that is produced by cows: 85

Amount of dairy a child should consume each day: 2 to 3 cups

Amount of dairy an adult should consume each day: 3 cups

The world's top five milk producers: India, United States, China, Pakistan, and Brazil

Amount of milk produced each year by American dairy cows: 20 billion gal. (76 billion L)

Natural life expectancy of a cow: About 20 years

Life expectancy of most dairy cows: 3 to 4 years

Percent increase in milk production in cows given synthetic growth hormones: 11 to 40

Did you find the truth?

Dairy cows produce much more milk each day than is necessary to feed a calf.

Most milk and dairy products are produced on small family farms.

Resources

Books

Lassieur, Allison. *Dairy*. Mankato, MN: Amicus High Interest, 2015.

Minden, Ceciia. *Cows*. Ann Arbor, MI: Cherry Lake Publishing, 2010.

Visit this Scholastic Web site for more information about Milk:
★ www.factsfornow.scholastic.com
Enter the keyword **Milk**

Important Words

antibiotics (an-tuh-bye-AH-tiks) drugs that are used to kill harmful bacteria and cure infections

conventional (kuhn-VEHN-shuh-nul) traditional

domesticated (duh-MEHS-ti-kay-tid) tamed, especially by generations of breeding, to live in close association with human beings as a pet or work animal

homogenized (huh-MAH-juh-nized) milk or cream that has been prepared by reducing the size of the fat globules to distribute them equally throughout

hormones (HOR-mohnz) natural substances that are produced in the body and influence the way the body grows or develops

lactose intolerance (LAK-tohs in-TAHL-ur-uhns) an inability to digest lactose, the sugar that is present in milk

mammals (MA-muhlz) a type of animal that feeds milk to its young and usually has hair or fur covering most of its skin

organic (or-GAN-ik) grown or made without the use of artificial chemicals

pasteurization (pas-chur-ih-ZAY-shuhn) the process of heating a liquid to a temperature high enough to kill many harmful germs, and then cooling it rapidly

udder (UH-dur) the bag-shaped part of a cow, goat, or other mammal that hangs below the belly and produces milk

Index

Page numbers in **bold** indicate illustrations.

About the Author

Ann O. Squire is a psychologist and an animal behaviorist. Before becoming a writer, she studied the behavior of rats, tropical fish in the Caribbean, and electric fish from central Africa. Her favorite part of being a writer is the chance to learn as much as she can about all sorts of topics. In addition to *Milk* and other books in the Farm to Table series, Dr. Squire has written about many different animals, from lemmings to leopards and cicadas to cheetahs. She lives in Asheville, North Carolina.